SPARKLY STICKER BOOK

# Bible Stories

KREGEL CHILDREN'S

These are the stickers you will need for this page.
whale
seahorse
jellyfish
clownfish
crab

# God Makes Animals and People

In the beginning, God made the world. He made many animals. The animals all had a home in the sea or on land. God also made people. Everything God made was fantastic!

*Genesis 1-2*

parrot
panda
girl
hen
ark

# God Kept Noah and the Animals Safe in the Ark

A flood was on the way. God told Noah to take his family and all kinds of animals into a big boat. They were safe inside. When they came out, God put a big, colorful rainbow in the sky. It was His promise to never destroy the world again by flood.

*Genesis 6-8*

# God Gives Abraham a Family

Abraham and Sarah wanted kids, but they had none. God said that they would have a big family. God's promise came true when Isaac was born. After Isaac, their family got bigger and bigger. Abraham and Sarah were very grateful to God.

*Genesis 15-21*

pillow
bird
moon
donkey
Isaac

# Joseph Forgives His Brothers

Joseph's brothers were cruel to him because he annoyed them by talking about his dreams. But God kept him safe. Later, Joseph not only forgave his brothers, but also saved them because there was not enough food in the land.

*Genesis 37*

grain
cat
head covering
palace
bottle

# God Uses Moses to Free His People

Moses came from a family of slaves. When he was a baby, the princess of Egypt found him. She took him in and he became a prince. Later in life, God told Moses to free the slaves, and with God's help, he did!

*Exodus 2-14*

boy
staff
squid
starfish
octopus

# Jesus Comes to Earth

More than 2000 years ago, Jesus was born. Wise men came to visit. They knew He was the Son of God. Jesus grew up and started telling people about God. He had many friends who followed Him everywhere.

*Luke 2 and Matthew 4*

trees
disciple
well
oranges
Jesus

# Jesus Loves You

Jesus showed that God loves everybody. God loves all children. God loves you! God even loves the ones everyone else hates, like Zacchaeus up in the tree.

*Matthew 14 and Luke 19*

cat
Jesus
butterfly
Zacchaeus
logs

# Jesus Dies and Rises Again

Jesus never did anything wrong. He died on the cross and rose up from the dead 3 days later. He took our sins away. Someday we can live with Jesus in heaven!

*John 3 and Matthew 28*